This Journal Belongs to:

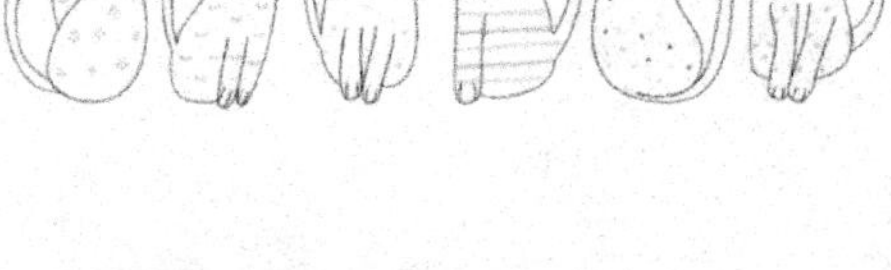

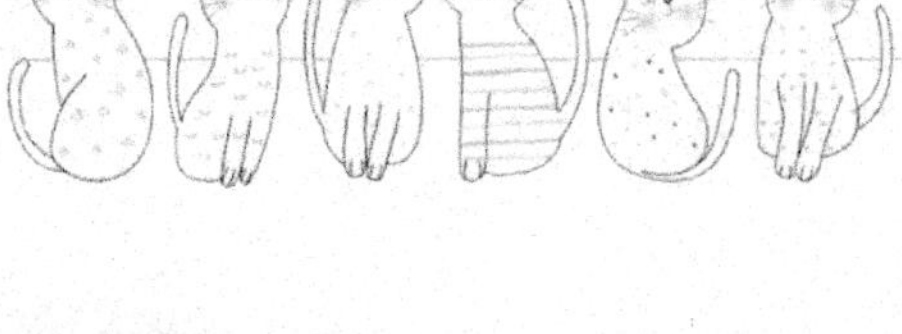

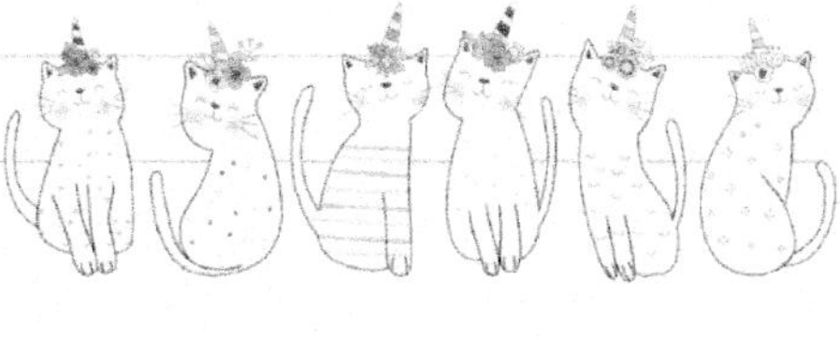

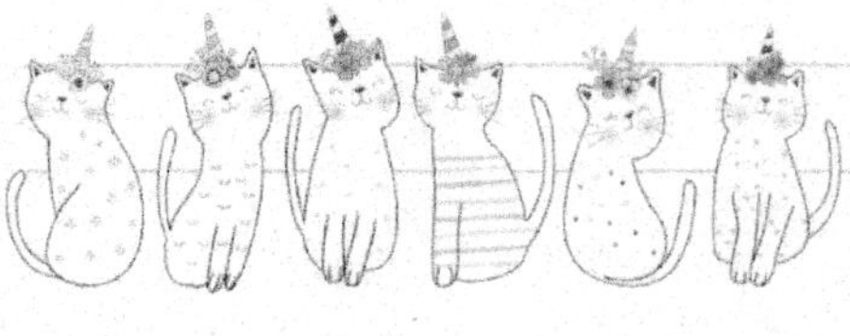

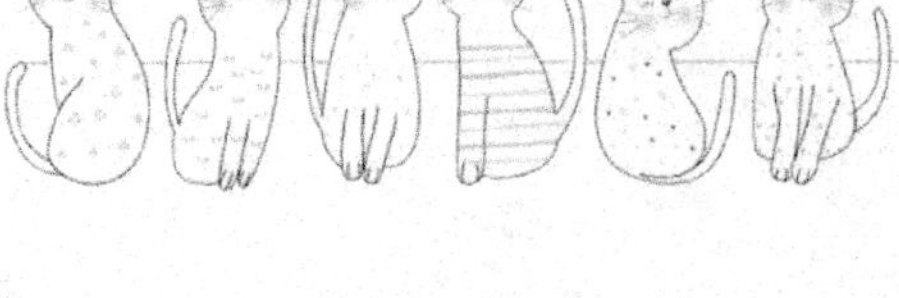

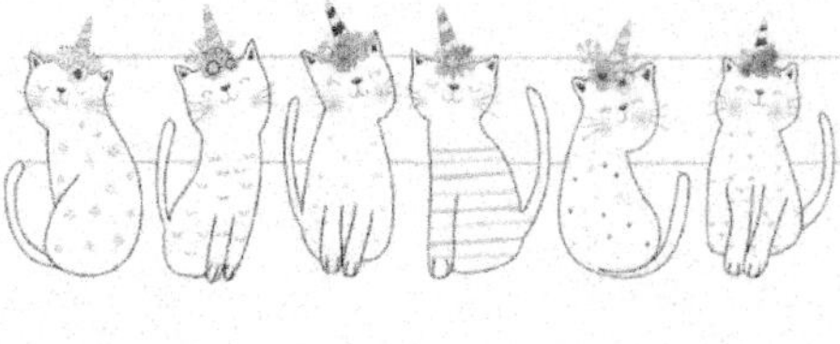

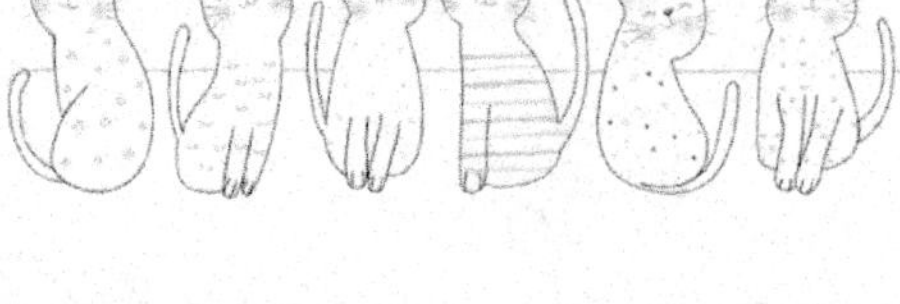

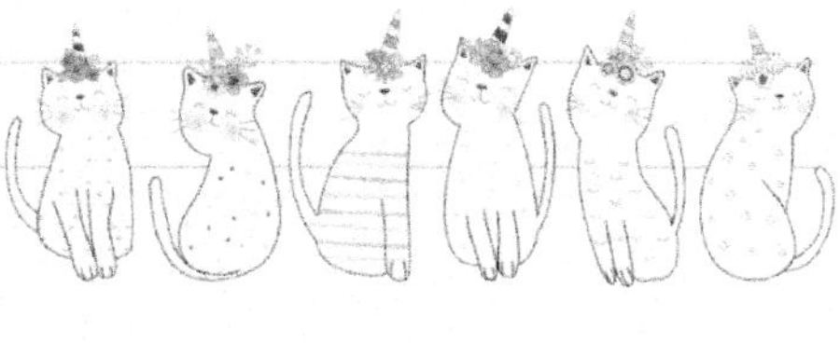

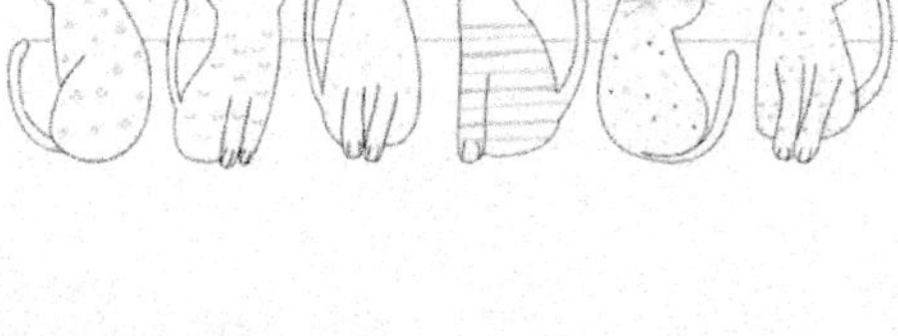

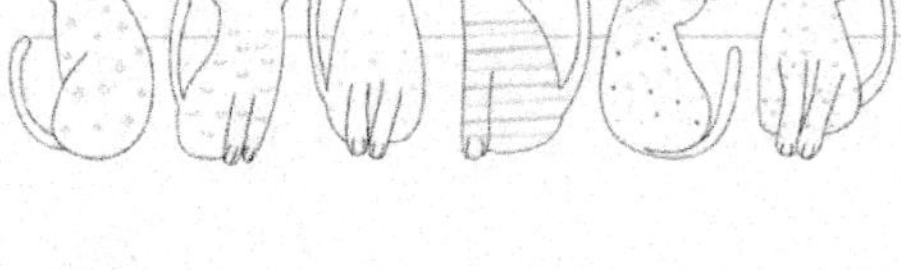

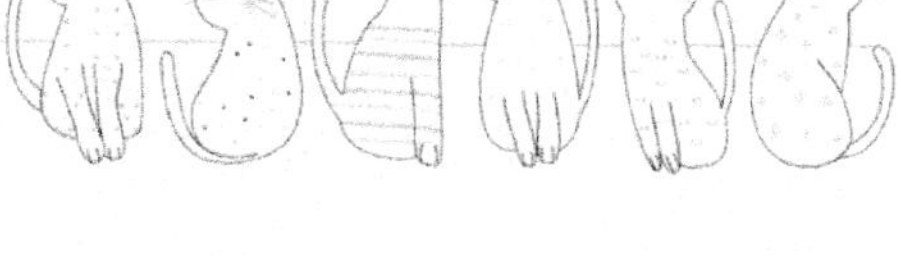

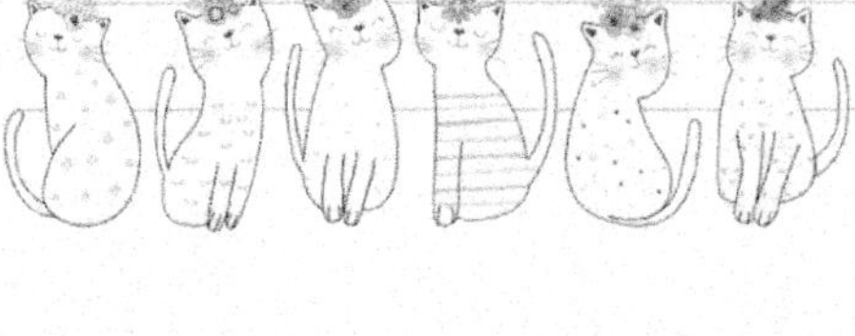

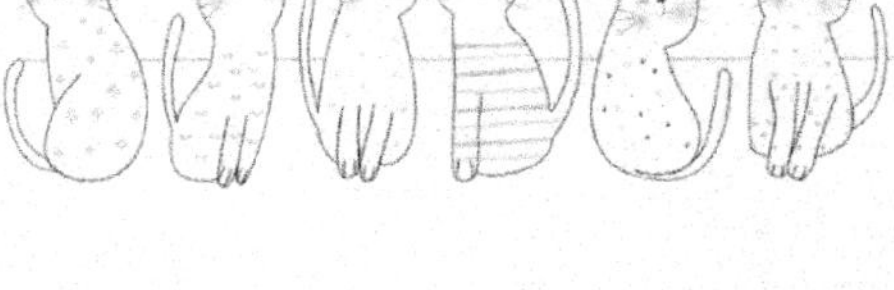

Made in the USA
Monee, IL
28 July 2022

10499740R00073